ULTIMATE CARS

Jaguar

Rob Scott Colson

WAYLAND

First published in 2009 by Wayland

Copyright © Wayland 2009

Wayland
338 Euston Road
London NW1 3BH

Wayland Australia
Level 17/207 Kent Street
Sydney NSW 2000

Editor: Camilla Lloyd
Produced by Tall Tree Ltd
Editor, Tall Tree: Emma Marriott
Designer: Jonathan Vipond

British Library Cataloguing in Publication Data

Colson, Robert Scott.
   Jaguar. -- (Ultimate cars)
   1. Jaguar automobile--Juvenile literature.
   I. Title II. Series
   629.2'222-dc22

ISBN: 978 0 7502 5721 3

Printed in China

Wayland is a division of Hachette Children's
Books, an Hachette UK company.

www.hachette.co.uk

Picture credits
All images Jaguar Cars, except:
4 AFP/Getty Images, 5b Magnus Manske,
13t Manwolste/Dreamstime.com,
13b Raysie/Dreamstime.com,
15b Motoring Picture Library/Alamy,
16l Stephen Foskett/GNU,
16–17 Motoring Picture Library/Alamy,
17 Spooky2006/Dreamstime.com,
18 Gerhard van Ackeren ,
19 Typhoonski/Dreamstime.com,

Contents

Jaguar

The Jaguar car company was founded in Blackpool, England, in 1922 by two friends called William Lyons and William Walmsley. They originally named their company Swallow Sidecars.

At first they made sidecars that fitted onto the side of motorbikes to allow them to carry passengers. By the 1930s, the company was known as SS Cars and was making elegant sports cars.

The 100 Jaguar was the first car made by SS Cars to be called a Jaguar.

Assembly line

William Lyons once said, 'The car is the closest we come to making something that feels alive.' He believed that his cars should use the latest technology but always be built by skilled craftspeople.

Jaguar cars are now built in modern factories in Birmingham and Liverpool.

Logo

SS Cars was officially renamed Jaguar in 1945. The name SS was by then associated with Adolf Hitler's Nazi regime in Germany, where the Schutzstaffel (known as the SS) was a feared police and military organization. The SS logo was also very similar to the Nazi symbol as both included the outstretched wings of an eagle. The company changed its logo to the famous leaping jaguar that is attached to the bonnet of older models.

The distinctive leaping jaguar mascot.

XJ

The XJ is Jaguar's most famous car. It is a saloon, which means that it is a passenger car with four doors.

Until recently, saloons were heavy and used a lot of fuel. The latest XJ is much lighter than older models. This is because the car's chassis (the main structure of the car) is made entirely from the lightweight metal aluminium, rather than heavier steel.

The original XJ was called the XJ6 because its engine had six cylinders.

Classic shape

The first XJ was made in 1968. XJ is short for Experimental Jaguar, which was the name the engineers gave the car while they were designing it. The XJ range has been modernized several times since the first model was made, but it has always kept its basic profile. This is the shape people now expect of a Jaguar car.

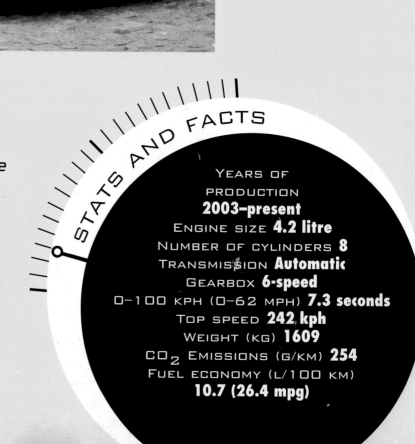

STATS AND FACTS

YEARS OF PRODUCTION
2003–present
ENGINE SIZE **4.2 litre**
NUMBER OF CYLINDERS **8**
TRANSMISSION **Automatic**
GEARBOX **6-speed**
0–100 KPH (0–62 MPH) **7.3 seconds**
TOP SPEED **242 kph**
WEIGHT (KG) **1609**
CO_2 EMISSIONS (G/KM) **254**
FUEL ECONOMY (L/100 KM)
10.7 (26.4 mpg)

A screen displays information about the car's performance from the XJ's on-board computer.

Amazing design

A car's suspension keeps the vehicle balanced as it travels over uneven ground. In the XJ, the suspension is controlled by a computer. The computer constantly checks the car's balance and makes tiny changes to the suspension springs. This ensures a smoother ride for passengers and also improves the car's aerodynamics (the way it cuts through the air).

The latest model of the XJ has a powerful eight-cylinder engine.

XK

The XK is a grand tourer, which is a two-seater sports car designed to be driven long distances.

This is a high-performance car, which can accelerate quickly and reach very high speeds. A limited-edition version of the XK, the XKR-S, is the fastest car Jaguar currently makes. Its speed is limited to 280 kph for safety reasons.

STATS AND FACTS

YEARS OF PRODUCTION **2007–present**
ENGINE SIZE **4.2 litre**
NUMBER OF CYLINDERS **8**
TRANSMISSION **Automatic**
GEARBOX **6-speed**
0–100 KPH (0–62 MPH) **6.1 seconds**
TOP SPEED **Limited to 250 kph**
WEIGHT (KG) **1595**
CO_2 EMISSIONS (G/KM) **269**
FUEL ECONOMY (L/100 KM) **11.3 (25 mpg)**

The XKR-S has been limited to 200 cars and is available only in Europe.

On the racetrack

Special racing versions, known as XKR GT3s, compete on the racetrack in the FIA GT3 European Championship. This is a series of races for cars that are similar to normal road cars. XKR GT3s also compete in the Britcar series of endurance races, where drivers attempt to drive as far as they can in a fixed time period.

The bar at the back of the XKR GT3 is known as the spoiler. It changes the flow of air over the car so that the air pushes down at the back. This keeps the wheels firmly on the track and stops the car from taking off at high speeds!

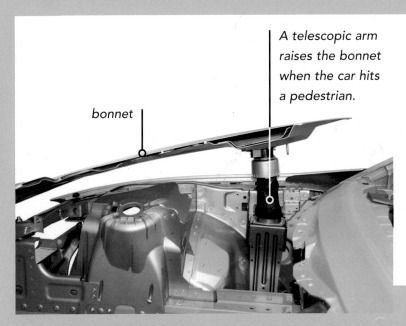

A telescopic arm raises the bonnet when the car hits a pedestrian.

bonnet

Amazing design

When a car hits a pedestrian, the most severe injuries often occur when the person's head dents the thin metal of the bonnet and hits the hard, solid engine underneath. The XK's Pedestrian Deployment Bonnet System (PDBS) senses when the car has hit someone and raises the bonnet away from the engine block. This high-tech system could save many lives.

XF

The newest Jaguar model is a mid-size sports sedan, which is a four-door car like a saloon but with some of the speed and acceleration of a sports car.

Traditionally, Jaguar cars have been more popular with men than women. Jaguar hopes the XF, with its emphasis on comfort and easy driving, will change this.

The Jaguar XF's entire body shape is designed to be as aerodynamic as possible.

Steering wheel

Cars have low gears for driving slowly, and high gears for driving at faster speeds. Changing gear in the Jaguar XF is made very easy by the Sequential Shift System. The driver moves a paddle mounted on the steering wheel, and the car's computer performs all the actions needed to change gear. This method of computerized control is known as 'drive-by-wire'.

Gear paddles

Amazing design

Today, cars are designed on computers, but designers still like to be able to touch a real model. Before the first working XF was made, test models known as prototypes were produced. To show what the main body of the car would look like, the designers made this full-size clay prototype.

STATS AND FACTS

YEARS OF PRODUCTION
2008–present
ENGINE SIZE **4.2 litre**
NUMBER OF CYLINDERS **8**
TRANSMISSION **Automatic**
GEARBOX **6-speed**
0–100 KPH (0–62 MPH) **5.1 seconds**
TOP SPEED **250 kph**
WEIGHT (KG) **1842**
CO_2 EMISSIONS (G/KM) **299**
FUEL ECONOMY (L/100 KM)
12.6 (22.4 mpg)

E-Type

When he first saw one, Enzo Ferrari, founder of Ferrari cars, is said to have called the Jaguar E-Type 'the most beautiful car ever made'. Many people in the 1960s agreed with him.

The E-Type is a grand tourer. It was not only more beautiful than most other grand tourers, it was also cheaper to buy. It was a hugely popular car and over 70,000 were made in the 14 years it was in production.

The E-Type has become an icon of 1960s motoring.

Amazing design

The E-Type's distinctive long, tubular body was designed by the engineer Malcolm Sayer. He developed new mathematical formulae to draw curves, making this kind of design possible for the first time. Sayer made all his calculations using just a pencil and paper. Today all the maths used in design is worked out by computer.

The impressive XK engine powered the E-Type.

The engine

The E-Type was powered by Jaguar's XK engine, which was first developed in the 1940s for luxury saloons and cars that took part in endurance races. The XK engine was so well designed that it was manufactured right up to 1994. It was powerful and very reliable, but also heavy, and was eventually replaced by modern, lighter engines.

STATS AND FACTS

YEARS OF PRODUCTION **1961–75**
ENGINE SIZE **4.2 litre**
NUMBER OF CYLINDERS **6**
TRANSMISSION **Manual**
GEARBOX **4-speed**
0–100 KPH (0–62 MPH) **7 seconds**
TOP SPEED **240 kph**
WEIGHT (KG) **1292**
CO_2 EMISSIONS (G/KM) **Not available**
FUEL ECONOMY (L/100 KM)
13.3 (21.3 mpg)

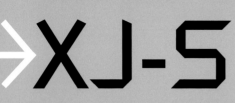

XJ-S

The replacement of the E-Type had none of its pleasing curves, but was even more aerodynamic.

The XJ-S had a huge 12-cylinder engine. The engines in the most powerful models were a massive 6 litres. To fit such a large engine at the front of the car, the XJ-S had a very long bonnet.

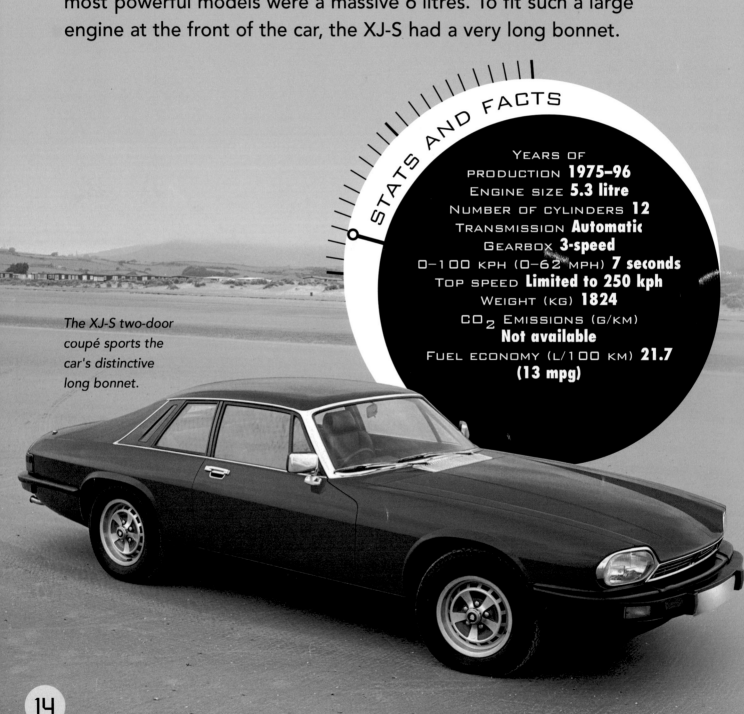

The XJ-S two-door coupé sports the car's distinctive long bonnet.

STATS AND FACTS

YEARS OF PRODUCTION **1975–96**
ENGINE SIZE **5.3 litre**
NUMBER OF CYLINDERS **12**
TRANSMISSION **Automatic**
GEARBOX **3-speed**
0–100 KPH (0–62 MPH) **7 seconds**
TOP SPEED **Limited to 250 kph**
WEIGHT (KG) **1824**
CO_2 EMISSIONS (G/KM) **Not available**
FUEL ECONOMY (L/100 KM) **21.7 (13 mpg)**

The 'flying buttresses' are a key feature of the XJ-S.

Amazing design

Arched sheets of metal extend from the top of each side of the rear window down along the sides of the boot. They are popularly called the XJ-S's 'flying buttresses'. Flying buttresses are features in buildings, such as cathedrals, that extend away from walls to help keep the building standing. The XJ-S's flying buttresses add to the overall strength of the chassis. When the car first came out, it was criticized for this design, but it is now the car's most recognizable feature.

Stripped down

The XJ-S is a grand tourer, so it is fitted with many features to provide comfort for the driver and passenger, such as air-conditioning and electric windows. These features all add to the weight of the car and slow it down. By stripping the car of its luxuries, it becomes over 200 kg lighter and can accelerate from 0 to 100 km just over a second more quickly.

XJ220

At the time it was made, the Jaguar XJ220 was the fastest production car (a car that can be bought by the public) ever made.

The car's name refers to its supposed top speed, 220 mph (350 kph). The idea for such a 'supercar' was first developed by a group of Jaguar employees in their spare time. The company was impressed by the group's plan, and in 1988, they started a project to build it.

The engine is visible through the rear window.

Better balance

The XJ220 is a mid-engine car, which means that the engine is just behind the driver. This distributes weight across all four wheels more evenly than a car with the engine at the front. Better balance allows the car to go even faster.

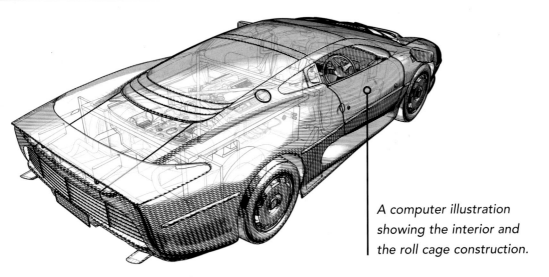

A computer illustration showing the interior and the roll cage construction.

Amazing design

Between the chassis and the driver of the XJ220 is a strong steel frame known as a roll cage. The cage protects the driver in the event of the car overturning at high speed. Cars used to race on the track are fitted with roll cages. Many features from racing cars were included in the XJ220's design by chief engineer Tom Walkinshaw, who also designed Formula 1 cars.

A total of 281 XJ220s were made.

STATS AND FACTS

YEARS OF PRODUCTION **1992–94**
ENGINE SIZE **3.5 litre**
NUMBER OF CYLINDERS **6**
TRANSMISSION **Manual**
GEARBOX **5-speed**
0–100 KPH (0–62 MPH) **3.9 seconds**
TOP SPEED **354 kph**
WEIGHT (KG) **1560**
CO_2 EMISSIONS (G/KM) **Not available**
FUEL ECONOMY (L/100 KM) **13.5 (21mpg)**

Daimler

The most expensive luxury saloon models in the Jaguar range are the Daimlers.

These models are named after a British company called Daimler, a luxury car manufacturer that was taken over by Jaguar in 1960. Daimlers were widely used by British Royalty, and royal weddings or funerals would often feature long rows of Daimler Limousines.

The dependable Daimler Sovereign was first introduced in 1966.

Daimler Sovereign

In the 1960s, the name Jaguar stood for the style and speed of the E-Type. It became associated with the changing trends in style and culture known as the Swinging Sixties. The Daimler Sovereign, on the other hand, as a solid and dependable version of the 420 series, was the choice of the city businessman who prided respectability over sportiness.

YEARS OF
PRODUCTION **1968–92**
ENGINE SIZE **4.2 litre**
NUMBER OF CYLINDERS **6**
TRANSMISSION **Automatic**
GEARBOX **3-speed**
0–100 KPH (0–62 MPH) **12 seconds**
TOP SPEED **175 kph**
WEIGHT (KG) **2133**
CO_2 EMISSIONS (G/KM) **Not available**
FUEL ECONOMY (L/100 KM)
18.8 (15mpg)

The passengers of a DS 420, or Daimler Limousine, sat in opulent comfort. The rear bench-seat spanned over 1.8 metres, and the dimensions of the car were the same as those of the Rolls-Royce Phantom VI.

Le Mans

Jaguar has a long history of success in motor racing, especially in endurance races.

The most famous endurance race of all is the Le Mans 24 Hours, which is held once a year at Le Mans, France. Cars with teams of two or three drivers race around the 13.6-km circuit, and whoever has completed the most circuits in 24 hours is the winner.

Race to win

During the 1950s, Jaguar cars dominated at Le Mans, winning the race first with the C-Type in 1951 and 1953, and then with the D-Type in 1955, '56 and '57. Both cars used Jaguar's XK engine, and this was the key to their success. When other manufacturers improved their engines, Jaguar stopped competing at Le Mans. They returned to the race in the 1980s with the XJR-9, and won it in 1988 and 1990. The winning D-Type in 1957 drove 4397 km. In 1988, the XJR-9 covered 5333 km.

The Jaguar C-Type was sold between 1951 and 1953, and a total of 52 were produced. The 'C' stood for 'competition' as there were no 'A-Type' or 'B-Type' Jaguars. It was followed, nonetheless, by the D-Type and the E-Type.

D-Type Jaguars were built from 1954 to 1957.

Amazing design

The D-Type was designed for racing, but it was also legal to drive it on the road. Its long, tube-like chassis was made as one piece, rather than a body stretched over a separate frame. This strong, aerodynamic construction method was copied from aircraft design. It is a method known as monocoque (French for 'single shell').

STATS AND FACTS

XJR-9
YEARS OF PRODUCTION
1988
ENGINE SIZE **7 litre**
NUMBER OF CYLINDERS **12**
TRANSMISSION **Manual**
GEARBOX **5-speed**
0–100 KPH (0–62 MPH) **3.1 seconds**
TOP SPEED **395 kph**
WEIGHT (KG) **881**
CO_2 EMISSIONS (G/KM) **Not available**
FUEL ECONOMY (L/100 KM)
Not available

In 1988, the Jaguar XJR-9 won Le Mans for the first time in 31 years.

Glossary

aerodynamic
Shaped to minimize air resistance when moving at high speed.

chassis
The frame of the car to which the body and the engine are attached.

clutch
A means of disconnecting the engine from the wheels in order to change gear.

coupé
A car with a hard roof that cannot be removed.

cylinder
A chamber in an engine inside which pistons pump up and down.

endurance race
A race in which cars are driven as far as they can within a set time limit.

four-wheel drive
A car engine that powers all four wheels at the same time. This helps with control on different road surfaces and at high speeds.

fuel economy
The rate at which a car uses fuel. It is measured in litres per 100 kilometres or miles per gallon.

gear
A system of cogs that transfers power from the engine to the wheels. Low gears give extra power for acceleration and high gears are used for faster speeds.

grand tourer
A sports car that is designed to be driven long distances. The name is a translation of the Italian term 'gran turismo'.

performance
A measurement of a car's power and handling. A car that accelerates quickly and has a high top speed is said to be high-performance.

production car
A car that is made in small series or large numbers and offered for sale to the public.

saloon (or sedan)
Usually a four-door car, with room for adult passengers in the rear. Sedan is the US term for saloon.

spoiler
A bar at the back of a car that interrupts the flow of air over the car, producing downforce that stops the car from leaving the road at high speeds or around corners.

suspension
A system of springs and shock absorbers that makes the ride smoother as the wheels pass over bumps.

transmission
The way in which a car transfers power from the engine to the wheels, via a gearbox that allows the driver to change gear.

Models at a glance

Model	Years Made	Numbers Built	Did You Know?
D-Type	1954–57	71	In 2008, the first factory production model of the D-Type sold at auction for £2.2 million.
E-Type	1961–75	70,000	Only 12 of the 'Lightweight' E-Type were built, making it an extremely rare and sought-after model.
Daimler DS 420	1968–92	4116	The DS 420 was widely used in the funeral trade, as both the relatives' car and the hearse for the deceased.
XJ	1968–present	98,500 (Series 1)	The name 'XJ' came from the car's code name during development, standing for 'Experimental Jaguar'.
XJ-S	1975–96	115,000	In the 1970s, the XJ-S featured in the television series *The New Avengers* and *Return of the Saint*.
XJ220	1992–94	281	The XJ220 had its own self-titled computer game and has appeared in a number of others.
XF	2008–present	100,000 per year	The XF has the best aerodynamic performance of any Jaguar car.

Websites

www.jaguar.com

The official website, with images and technical information on all the current models.

www.topgear.com

The website of the popular BBC TV series, with interactive games and clips from the show. They review all the Jaguar models, saying exactly what they like and don't like about them.

www.sportscarcup.com

A site that compares sports cars made by different companies. Includes photos, technical information and a short history of each model.

www.autosport.com

A wealth of information about all forms of motorsport, including rallying and endurance races.

Index

Contents of titles in series: